I'M A GLOBAL CITIZEN

Culture & Diversity

Written by Georgia Amson-Bradshaw

Illustrated by David Broadbent

Franklin Watts
Published in paperback in Great Britain in 2020 by The Watts Publishing Group
Copyright © The Watts Publishing Group, 2019

 Produced for Franklin Watts by
White-Thomson Publishing Ltd
www.wtpub.co.uk

Series Editor: Georgia Amson-Bradshaw
Series Designer: David Broadbent
All Illustrations by: David Broadbent

Printed in Dubai

Franklin Watts
An imprint of
Hachette Children's Group
Part of The Watts Publishing Group
Carmelite House
50 Victoria Embankment
London EC4Y 0DZ

An Hachette UK Company
www.hachette.co.uk
www.franklinwatts.co.uk

 MIX
Paper from
responsible sources
FSC® C104740

Facts, figures and dates were correct when going to press.

CONTENTS

Look out for this little book symbol to find definitions of important words. Other definitions can be found in the glossary on page 30.

What is culture?

Culture is a word that describes a group of people's 'way of life'. It includes all sorts of things, such as what a particular group of people wear, what they eat, their language, their religion and beliefs, their holidays and special occasions.

Global culture

Culture is passed on from one generation to the next, but it isn't anything to do with genetics. It is something we learn, not something we are born with. Here are some examples of cultural habits around the world.

Decorating your hand with henna

Letting off fireworks on 4 July

Worshipping in the mosque

olá

Speaking Portuguese

You might notice that some of these examples are linked with one particular country, such as US Independence Day celebrations on 4 July. Other examples, such as going to the mosque, which is part of practising the religion of Islam, are done by people in many different countries.

Drinking tea

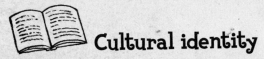

Cultural identity

Your cultural identity has many different parts to it. You will share some of them with many people who don't entirely share your culture. But adding all the different bits together – the dishes you eat, the clothes you wear, the things you believe – gives you your cultural identity.

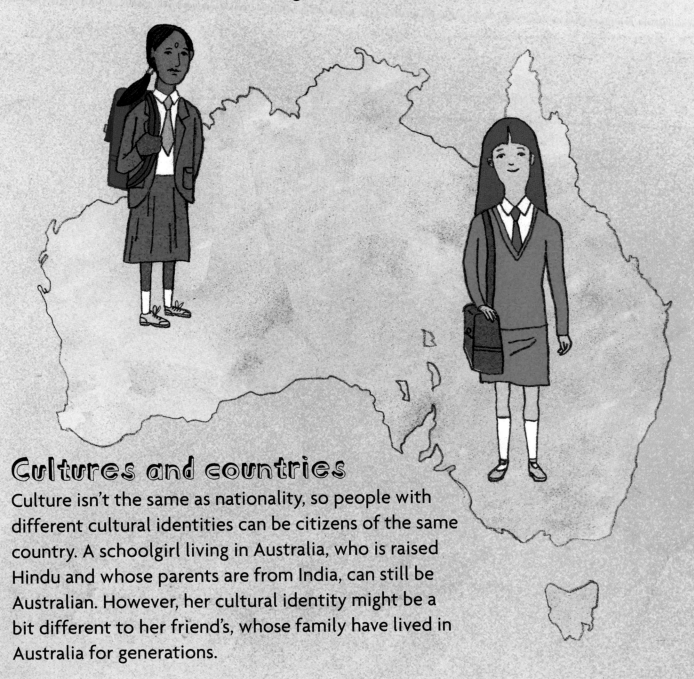

Cultures and countries

Culture isn't the same as nationality, so people with different cultural identities can be citizens of the same country. A schoolgirl living in Australia, who is raised Hindu and whose parents are from India, can still be Australian. However, her cultural identity might be a bit different to her friend's, whose family have lived in Australia for generations.

What is diversity?

When a place or an organisation such as a school contains lots of different kinds of people, including people with disabilities, different cultural identities and people of different races, we say it is diverse.

Race

We use the term 'race' when we are talking about people's physical features, such as the colour of their skin and the shape of their face. Two people with the same cultural identity can be of different races. Two people of the same race can have different cultural identities.

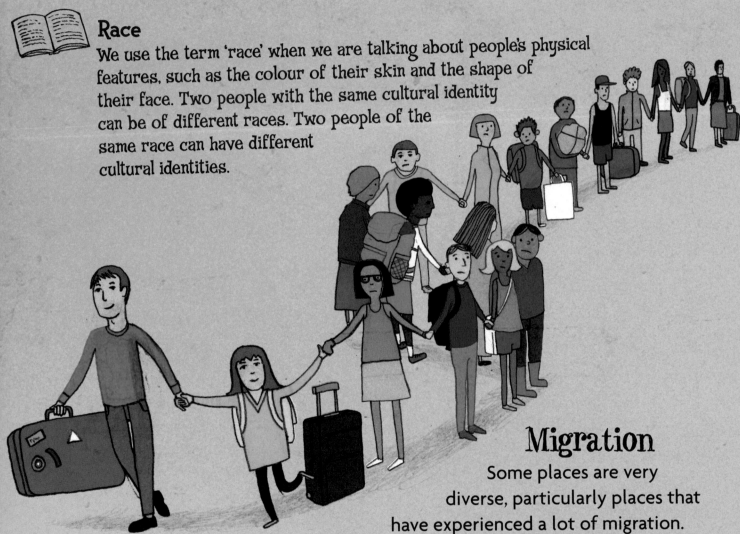

Migration

Some places are very diverse, particularly places that have experienced a lot of migration. Migration is when people move from one country or place to another, often to look for work or a better quality of life. Big cities are often diverse, because the wide range of jobs and other opportunities attract people from all around the world.

Benefits of diversity

Having a mixture of people with different experiences, abilities and viewpoints benefits organisations or societies, when people respect and listen to one another. This is because people can bring their different perspectives and ways of thinking together, and come up with creative ideas and solutions to problems.

Studies have shown that businesses with more diverse workforces are more successful, and that students work better in schools that have a diverse group of pupils. Getting to know people from different backgrounds helps us grow, understand new ways of living and experience life to the fullest.

Can you think of any occasions when you have learnt something from someone who has a different background to you?

what's YOUR culture?

Make a culture self-portrait. Find a piece of paper and some colouring pencils, and draw a picture of yourself in the middle. Around the edges, draw and write some of the following things:

Food

Which three foods do you and your family eat most often? Are there any foods such as bread or rice that you eat almost every day? Which foods do you only ever eat on special occasions such as birthdays or holidays?

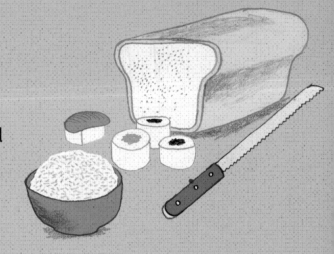

Beliefs

Do you follow a religion or believe in God? If so, how do you practise your religion? Do you pray or go to any regular services? Are there any objects related to your beliefs?

clothes

Do you wear the same kinds of clothes as most people in your local area? If the answer is yes, which pieces of clothing do you see a lot of people wearing — jeans or collared shirts, for example? What do you wear on special occasions?

Festivals

What are the most exciting special occasions for you in the year? How are they celebrated? Are they religious holidays or something else?

Values

Our values are what give us our sense of right and wrong. They are the things that we think are most important in life, in our own behaviour and others'. Kindness, putting family first, honesty, bravery, being respectful and being open-minded are all values. Come up with as many values as you can. Now try and list them in order of importance to you.

Language

Which language or languages do you speak? For some people, being able to speak a language that isn't the one most widely used in their country is an important part of their cultural identity.

Music and dance

What sort of music do you like? Do you know any dances?

Multicultural life

More than ever before, people from different backgrounds and cultures live together in places all over the world. Sometimes people find it challenging when the behaviour or attitudes of their new neighbours is different to their own. But when we make an effort to understand one another, we all benefit.

Mix of cultures

Think about the place where you live, or a city nearby. Are there restaurants serving food from other countries? Is there a mix of religious buildings? Are there shops selling objects or clothes from different cultures? Are any of your friends and neighbours originally from another country, or do they have parents who are?

Make a list of all the things that would be missing from your life without multiculturalism.

Cafe

POLSKI SMAK

Many people, many places

Some of the places with the greatest mix of cultures are big cities. For example, people of over 270 nationalities call London their home, around a third of New Yorkers were born abroad, and more that 250 languages are spoken by residents of Sydney!

But it isn't just western cities where multiculturalism is a part of everyday life. Many countries have a long history of multiculturalism – for example, Chad has 100 different registered ethnic groups and Zimbabwe has 16 official languages.

In fact, the world's 20 most culturally diverse countries are in Africa. Elsewhere, Singapore is the most religiously diverse country and Papua New Guinea has the highest number of languages spoken – a whopping 820!

Indian Spice

Prejudice and discrimination

Has anyone ever wrongly assumed you wouldn't understand something, just because you were a kid? Prejudice means to pre-judge someone without really knowing them.

Making assumptions

People can be prejudiced about all sorts of different things, such as someone's age, their weight, where they are from, what religion they are or whether they are a boy or a girl. Whatever the reason, prejudice means having a negative attitude towards a person or a group of people based on an assumption of what they are like.

Discrimination

Prejudice is an opinion or an attitude. Discrimination is when that prejudice is acted on. For example, if an employer is prejudiced against overweight people and believes they are all lazy, he might discriminate against an overweight job applicant by not hiring them, even if they are the most experienced person who applied.

Race and religion

Prejudice on the basis of race, such as thinking that people of one race are naturally more intelligent, hard-working or better than another is called racism. Another type of prejudice is on the basis of religion. Prejudice against Muslims is called Islamophobia. Prejudice against Jewish people is called anti-Semitism.

Impacts of prejudice

In its most extreme forms, prejudice is used to justify extremely cruel or violent acts, such as forcing black people into slavery in the USA and Europe from the sixteenth to the nineteenth centuries, or the systematic killing of Jewish people during the Second World War (1939–1945).

More often, prejudice and discrimination are less extreme. They can include acts such as calling people rude names, not wanting to work with them, assuming someone is from another country because they have a different skin colour, or feeling afraid when seeing someone in the street wearing religious clothing.

Discrimination in society

Some societies officially discriminate against certain groups of people. In other places, discrimination is not legally supposed to take place, but it still does, and has a huge impact on people's lives.

Segregation

In the USA and South Africa, black people used to be officially discriminated against by laws that said they had to attend separate, poorer-quality schools, use separate facilities, sit at the back of buses and live in poorer-quality housing than white people. In the USA, this was called segregation. In South Africa, it was part of a system called apartheid. Read more about apartheid on pages 22–23.

Unofficial discrimination

For people who don't experience day-to-day racial or cultural discrimination, the fact that everyone officially has the same legal rights can lead them to believe that there is now a fair and level playing field. However, this is not the case.

Life chances

Many people are still discriminated against in important life events such as applying for a job, a house or a bank loan. For example, a study in the United Kingdom sent out almost-identical CVs with different names randomly assigned. The applicants with 'white-sounding' names were 74 per cent more likely to receive a positive response than those with 'ethnic minority' names.

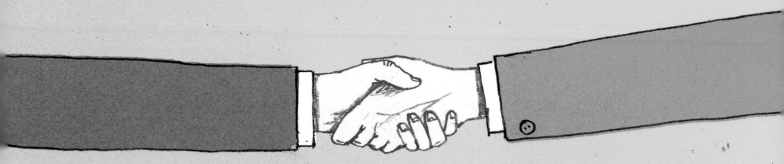

The police and legal system also often unfairly target and punish people based on their race or culture. In England and Wales, people from Black and Minority Ethnic (BAME) groups are twice as likely as white people to be stopped and searched by police. People from BAME communities are also more likely to be given prison sentences than white people convicted of similar crimes, and to receive longer sentences.

where on Earth?

NIGERIA

How much do you think you know about other places and cultures around the world? Try this quiz to find out. And remember, sometimes our ideas about a place aren't always exactly accurate!

SYRIA

Each of these facts is true for one of **THREE** countries; the **United Kingdom, Nigeria and Syria**. Can you figure out which country each fact is true for?

UK

1. This country has two official languages.

2. This country has 99 universities.

3. One of the oldest cities in the world is in this country.

4. This country has a film industry worth billions of dollars.

5. The king or queen of this country is also the head of the country's religion.

6. Roughly half the population of this country are Christian, and half are Muslim.

7. Football and basketball are the most popular sports in this country.

8. This country has six World Heritage Sites – globally important places to natural or cultural heritage.

9. Four million children are living in poverty in this country.

Check the answers on page 32. Did any of them surprise you? Often, the media (that's things such as TV and books) only shows us one side of a place. That can create stereotypes, such as 'everyone in Africa is poor'. These are oversimplified and inaccurate ideas of places or people that can lead to prejudice.

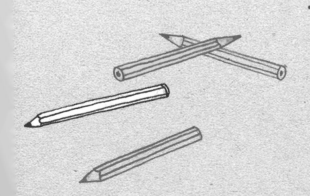

Why not find out more about each of these countries, and design posters describing the culture and landscape of each country?

Seeing things differently

Learning about other cultures is interesting, and it helps us avoid misunderstandings when we meet new people. Visiting different countries and getting to know people from different cultures helps us to understand what we have in common. Often, our idea of other places and cultures comes from what we read or see on TV, but this doesn't always show the whole picture.

Seen on screen

The media often isn't very good at showing and celebrating cultural differences. We've looked at how what we learn from the media about other countries and cultures can be stereotypes rather than reality – but not showing different nationalities, cultures and races at all also has an effect.

Think of your favourite hero from a book or a film. What is their culture or race? Is it the same as yours?

Seeing yourself

When people of different races and cultures are not shown in the media, it is a way of leaving people out. For people who are left out, not ever seeing people who look like them on screen and in books can make them feel like they are weird or different, and can hurt their self-esteem.

It can also increase prejudiced opinions in people from the majority culture, because they don't see people who are different from them in important roles.

Challenge

Draw a picture of one of your favourite characters – but give them a different cultural identity or race. Now write a new story featuring them, but set it in a different country. Try to show the country in a way that isn't a stereotype.

Wheel of life chances

The impact of discrimination on people from minority races and cultures can be felt in a lot of different ways, but it isn't always obvious from the outside because everybody gets lucky and unlucky sometimes.

RULES:

1. Find a die and a friend to play the Wheel of Life Chances.
2. One person plays as the minority group member, and one as the majority group member.
3. Move around the segments from 1 to 4. At each segment, both players roll the die once. If your number comes up, get a point. If no one's numbers come up, no one gets a point.
4. The person with the **fewest** points at the end wins.

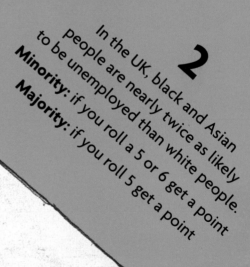

1

In the USA, black students are more than three times more likely to be excluded from school than white students, often for the same behaviour.

Minority: if you roll a 1, 2 or 3 get a point

Majority: if you roll a 1 get a point

2

In the UK, black and Asian people are nearly twice as likely to be unemployed than white people.

Minority: if you roll a 5 or 6 get a point

Majority: if you roll 5 get a point

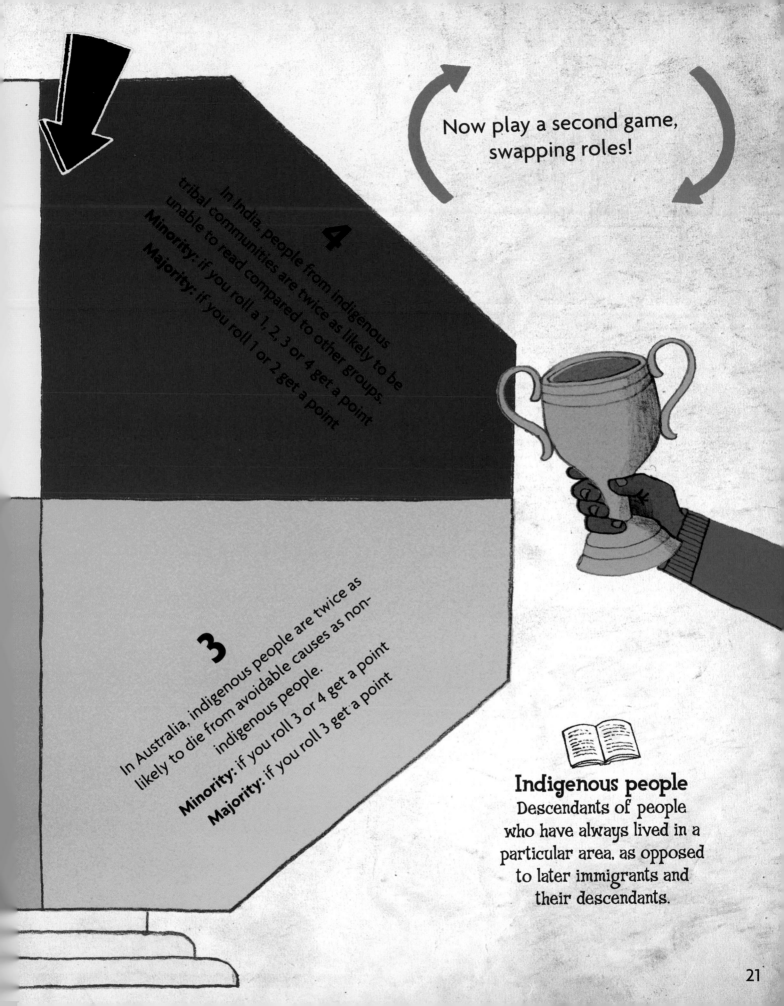

Now play a second game, swapping roles!

4

In India, people from indigenous tribal communities are twice as likely to be unable to read compared to other groups.

Minority: if you roll a 1, 2, 3 or 4 get a point

Majority: if you roll 1 or 2 get a point

3

In Australia, indigenous people are twice as likely to die from avoidable causes as non-indigenous people.

Minority: if you roll 3 or 4 get a point

Majority: if you roll 3 get a point

Indigenous people

Descendants of people who have always lived in a particular area, as opposed to later immigrants and their descendants.

Making change happen: Apartheid in South Africa

Apartheid means 'apartness'. It was the name of a system in South Africa that was put in place in 1948 by the ruling Nationalist Party. It separated people based on their race. Although black people had been treated as second-class citizens in South Africa for centuries, apartheid made it official law.

No rights

White people and black people were forced to live and work apart from each other. Despite there being more black people in South Africa than white people, apartheid gave white people all the power. Black people were not allowed to vote, or travel in white areas without special papers. Those caught breaking the law were put in prison.

Protest and tactics

Several protest groups campaigned against apartheid. One of them was the African National Congress, or ANC. They organised non-violent demonstrations, mass strikes and campaigns. Then, in 1960, 69 protestors were massacred at a demonstration in Sharpeville by the police.

FREEDOM

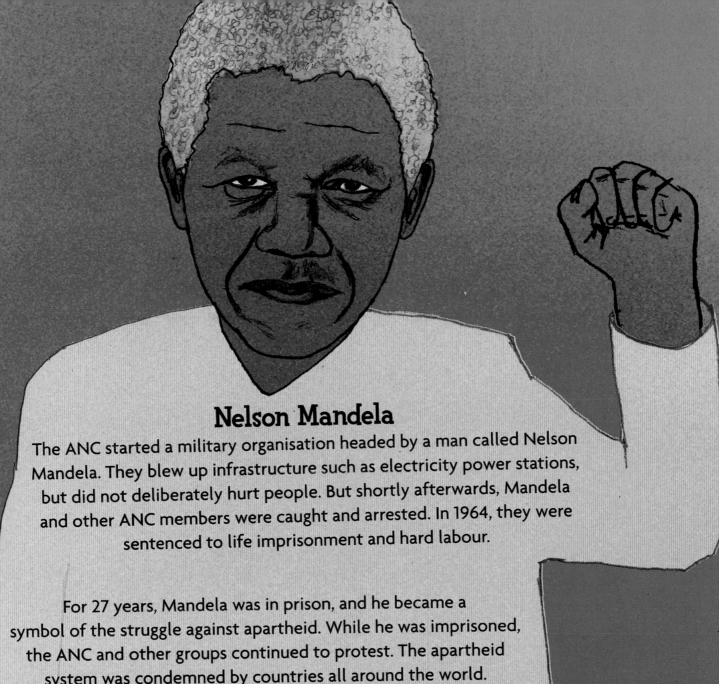

Nelson Mandela

The ANC started a military organisation headed by a man called Nelson Mandela. They blew up infrastructure such as electricity power stations, but did not deliberately hurt people. But shortly afterwards, Mandela and other ANC members were caught and arrested. In 1964, they were sentenced to life imprisonment and hard labour.

For 27 years, Mandela was in prison, and he became a symbol of the struggle against apartheid. While he was imprisoned, the ANC and other groups continued to protest. The apartheid system was condemned by countries all around the world.

The end of apartheid

In the early 1990s, after years of protest, unrest and international pressure, apartheid was brought to an end. Nelson Mandela was released from prison in 1990 and in 1994, a new election was held in which people of all races could vote. The ANC won the election and Nelson Mandela became president of South Africa.

Profile: Bolivia's 'Cholitas'

Bolivia is a small country in South America. In the sixteenth century, Spanish conquistadors (soldiers who conquered newly discovered countries) invaded and took over much of South America, ruling over the local, indigenous people.

The indigenous people rebelled against the Spanish rulers. In an attempt to break their spirits, the Spanish forced the local people to wear Spanish-style clothing. For women, this included a pleated skirt and petticoats called pollera, and a decorative shawl called a manta. But over time, the indigenous women in Bolivia embraced the clothing, and made it a style all of their own, later adding a bowler hat to the look.

Over time, inequality between people descended from the Spanish and people descended from indigenous people continued. The people with Spanish ancestors were mostly wealthier than those with indigenous ancestors, who also continued to wear the same style of clothing, as it became part of their cultural identity. They were given the nickname 'cholitas'.

The inequality between the groups meant that the cholita women, who were easily identified by their outfits, were often refused entry to certain restaurants, taxis and even some public buses. Considered lower class, it would not have been possible for a woman to be seen in cholita dress working in an office or in any position of power. Girls wearing cholita dress would not be allowed in school.

In the latter part of the twentieth century, grassroots groups of rural and indigenous people began to organise and gain power, and in 2005, Bolivia's first indigenous president was elected. Since then, the cholita style has become a symbol of national pride. Cholitas can now be found anchoring TV and radio programmes, working in the government and studying at university... as well as on the runway of the newly-popular cholita fashion shows!

Activate! Act against racism

Big problems such as racism and cultural discrimination can seem very difficult to solve. But even in the most extreme circumstances it is possible to change people's minds and in doing so, change the world. Here are some actions that we can all take as individuals to challenge racism and discrimination.

Say something

Speak up when someone is being racist, or when you see someone saying something mean or prejudiced. You don't have to be mean back, but you can still challenge them – ask 'Why would you say something like that?', or say 'That's not OK', if you feel safe to do so.

Make friends

Find a pen pal from a different culture or country and find out about their life. Make an effort to make friends with people who live near to you, but have different races or religions. Getting to know people is a very important way to break down barriers and prejudiced ideas. If you think your classmates don't know much about your culture, share some information about it with them.

Discuss it

Talk to your friends to find out how much they know about the issue. If they don't know a lot, share your knowledge with them. You could prepare a presentation to give to your class on the subject.

School rules

Find out what your school does to prevent bullying and racism. What are their policies around it? Are they taking action on the issue? If you don't think enough is being done, ask them to improve!

Take action

Join an organisation that works to reduce discrimination and supports human rights. You could organise a fundraiser for them, or see if a speaker from that organisation can come and do a talk at your school.

What other ideas can you come up with to act against racism and discrimination?

Organise!
Put on a culture day

Help your friends to understand and appreciate other cultures by throwing a world culture day at your school or club. Ask everyone to bring in some items, such as clothing, or activities either from their own culture, or from one that they have researched. It could be all sorts of things, such as the following:

Food

Get people to bring in a delicious dish for everyone to share. Turn it into an international picnic.

Music

Have everyone choose a tune and put a playlist together with music from all different cultures. Are there any dances that go with the tunes? If you can find a video of any dances online, you could host a workshop where people can learn the moves and then dance along.

Sport and games

Find out which sports and games are popular in other cultures. Is there one you haven't tried before? Read up on the rules and have a go at playing it.

Film screening

Which films and TV shows are popular in other cultures? Have an 'international cinema screening'. This could be a room where TV shows and films are shown – write up the screening schedule so people can decide which one they want to check out, and provide popcorn!

Arts and crafts

Set up an art corner. Have people bring in designs and pieces of art in styles from different cultures, and let people have a go at creating their own. Ask people to research not just what the art looks like, but how the style evolved and why it looks the way it does. Pin up the finished pieces on the wall as a gallery show.

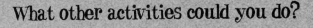

What other activities could you do?

Glossary

apartheid a racist system in South Africa that separated black and white people and meant white people had all the power and better living standards

discrimination treating someone unfairly because of assumptions you've made without really knowing them

diversity when there are lots of different kinds of people in a place or group, including people with different races, cultural identities and disabilities

ethnic minority a person or small group of people with a culture that is different to most of the people who live in the same place as them

generation the normal amount of time between a parent being born and their children being born

genetics how certain features, such as eye colour, are passed from parents to their offspring

grassroots describes people working for change on a local, face-to-face level

henna coloured dye used to decorate the body with patterns

heritage something that is handed down from the past and is part of your culture and background

human rights things that everyone must be allowed, no matter what country they live in – for example, the right to education and to be treated equally by the law

immigrant someone who moves from the country where they were born to another country to live there

indigenous people descendants of people who have always lived in a particular area

infrastructure the basic services – such as roads, electricity, water and sewage – that a society needs to work properly

mosque a Muslim place of worship where people go to pray and meet

multiculturalism people from lots of different cultures living together in one place

nationality describes the country in which you were born, or to which you moved to and became a legal citizen – for example, someone born in France is of French nationality

race a group of people that share some of the same physical features, such as skin colour

segregation splitting people into groups and making them live separately from each other, usually with one group treated better than the other

stereotype an overly simple, untrue idea that many people have about a group – for example, that men are bad at cooking and cleaning

strike stopping work in protest for more money, better working conditions or other changes

Further information

What is race? Who are racists? Why does skin colour matter? And other big questions
Claire Heuchan and Nikesh Shukla (Wayland, 2018)
This book explores the history of race and society, and discusses the damaging effects of stereotypes. It explores how we can spot and stand up to racism, and how to protect against and stop racist behaviour.

Who are refugees and migrants? What makes people leave their homes? And other big questions
Michael Rosen and Annemarie Young (Wayland, 2016)
In this book you can learn about the history of migration around the world and issues today. The book covers diversity, multiculturalism and the prejudice and discrimination that people can face.

Cultural issues (my life, your life)
by Honor Head (Franklin Watts, 2017)
This book looks at all sorts of cultural differences and traditions, including religion, diet, clothes and attitudes, and the different cultural pressures and challenges that can exist in people's lives.

Black History: Community and identity
Dan Lyndon (Franklin Watts, 2014)
This title in the Black History series looks at the growth of black communities across the world, and the strengthening of black identity.

Websites

www.bbc.com/education/topics/z7rrd2p/resources
Lots of short videos about exploring and respecting the different ways people live, from understanding disabilities to following a child refugee's journey to safety and a new start.

www.youtube.com/watch?v=mzu3ira61k8
A TEDx talk video from nine-year-old Maryam Elassar telling a personal story about learning to understand cultural differences and form new friendships.

www.youtube.com/watch?v=OoHdwUEfBts
Kid President's guide to making new friends, including how to talk to other young people about feeling different and accepting each other's differences.

Note to parents and teachers: every effort has been made by the Publishers to ensure websites are suitable for children, that they are of the highest educational value, and that they contain no inappropriate or offensive material. However, because of the nature of the Internet, it is impossible to guarantee that the contents of these sites will not be altered. We strongly advise that Internet access is supervised by a responsible adult.

Index

Answers to pages 16–17: 1. United Kingdom (English and Welsh), 2. Nigeria, 3. Syria (city of Aleppo), 4. Nigeria, 5. United Kingdom (the Queen is the head of the Church), 6. Nigeria, 7. Syria (although football is the most popular sport in the UK and Nigeria too), 8. Syria, 9. United Kingdom.